WRESTLING SUPERSTARS

AJ STYLES

By J. R. Kinley

Kaleidoscope

Minneapolis, MN

BIGFOOT BOOKS

The Quest for Discovery Never Ends

•••

This edition first published in 2020 by Kaleidoscope Publishing, Inc.

No part of this publication may be reproduced in whole or in part without written permission of the publisher.

For information regarding permission, write to Kaleidoscope Publishing, Inc. 6012 Blue Circle Drive Minnetonka, MN 55343

Library of Congress Control Number 2019940191

ISBN
978-1-64519-085-1 (library bound)
978-1-64494-222-2 (paperback)
978-1-64519-186-5 (ebook)

Printed in the United States of America.

FIND ME IF YOU CAN!

Bigfoot lurks within one of the images in this book. It's up to you to find him!

TABLE OF
CONTENTS

CHAPTER 1

SummerSlam

It is August 2016. The SummerSlam main event roars to a start. The air is hot. So is the sold-out crowd. The fans are split. Some support legend John Cena. Others like AJ Styles. Styles is skilled. But he is new to World Wrestling Entertainment (WWE). Styles needs to prove himself.

The fans are on their feet. The announcer gets people excited. He calls the wrestlers "two of the very best to lace up the boots." They come head-to-head. Styles starts the action with a dropkick. Then Cena lands a punch. It sends Styles to the **canvas**. He gets to his feet. But then Cena bounces him off the corner of the ring. Styles is down again.

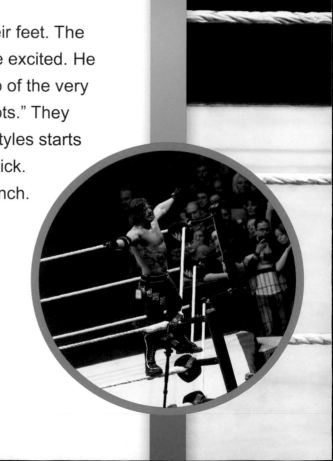

AJ Styles already had a successful wrestling career when he started wrestling in WWE, but he needed to defeat a legend like John Cena to prove himself.

The SummerSlam 2016 match between AJ Styles and John Cena was action-packed and intense.

Next, Cena tries his **signature** move. It's called the Attitude Adjustment. He lifts Styles onto his shoulders. But Styles throws his elbows out. He escapes. Styles locks his arms around Cena. He's going for a **suplex**! He slams Cena onto the **apron**. They both fall out of the ring. But they roll back in under the ropes.

Cena sends Styles into a back body drop. Styles goes down. The referee starts counting. The match will end if he gets to three. He reaches one. But Styles gets up. Cena pins him again for a two-count. Styles escapes. He lands a few punches. Cena sends him back to the canvas. He taunts Styles.

But Styles is determined. Cena lifts him on his shoulders. He's trying the Attitude Adjustment again. Cena throws him, but Styles lands on his feet. Styles goes for his finishing move. It's called the Styles Clash. He lifts Cena upside down. He smashes him into the mat. Styles thinks it could be over. But Cena breaks out of the pin. The crowd goes through the roof.

FUN FACT
Styles's match against Cena won Pro Wrestling Illustrated Match of the Year 2016.

COOL INK

AJ Styles has a large tattoo on his side. It has his initials. "AJ" is written in big letters. Below that are four dates. The dates are birthdays. They are the days when his children were born.

05-03-05
02-14-07
09-15-09
10-08-14

The wrestlers go back and forth. Cena tries to get Styles to give up. He traps Styles in a hold. But Styles turns the tables. He gets the upper hand again. They go through their moves. They're tired. Cena looks amazed at Styles's spirit.

Cena tries to lift Styles one last time. But Styles won't let him. He takes control. He does another Styles Clash. Then he flies off the ropes and into Cena. He ends the match with a **pinfall**. Styles wins! The match lasted more than twenty-three minutes. Cena exits the ring. He leaves his "Never Give Up" wristband on the canvas. Styles has proven himself worthy.

AJ Styles shows his fighting spirit by continuing to wrestle even when he's struggling.

CHAPTER 2

Finding a Calling

AJ Styles's real name is Allen Jones. But people call him AJ. He was born at a US military base. He went to high school in Georgia. He wrestled on the school team.

FUN FACT
All four of Styles's children have the initials A. J.

Styles got his start by wrestling in high school and college.

He improved his skills. Styles also did competitive cheerleading. That was how he learned to do flips. All the practice was worth it. Styles became a college wrestler.

In 1998, he decided to try professional wrestling. Two of his friends joined, too. They trained with National Championship Wrestling (NCW).

Styles remembers getting started. He took his first **bump**. That's when he thought, "I'm doing this for the rest of my life."

Soon, he knew he could be a pro wrestler. His ability to do flips came in handy. That skill got him matches. He was willing to learn from anyone. Styles worked side jobs while he trained. He earned money for his family. He drove an ambulance and delivered water. On weekends, he wrestled.

Early in his career, Styles's ability to do flips and other tricks got him matches.

Styles became known as the Phenomenal AJ Styles thanks to his impressive wrestling abilities.

WHAT'S IN A NAME?

AJ Styles wanted to be called Velocity. But he didn't get to wrestle under that name. He went by Mr. Olympia for one match. He also wrestled once as Air Styles. He didn't like the ring name AJ Styles at first. But it grew on him.

He soon began competing. At first, he wrestled as Mr. Olympia. Styles wore his old college wrestling uniform. He turned it inside out. And he wore a mask. He'd always wanted to do that. He lost his first match. But he kept working hard. Soon, he had a new name. A **promoter** named him AJ Styles. Styles competed a lot. He learned all he could. In 2002, he joined Total Nonstop Action Wrestling (TNA). He became known as the Phenomenal AJ Styles.

FUN FACT

AJ Styles first performed the Styles Clash on television in 2001.

CHAPTER 3

Sensational Moves

It's September 11, 2016. AJ Styles faces Dean Ambrose. They're competing for the WWE Championship. Styles wants to give the crowd an exciting match. His fans love seeing **sensational** action. They expect his signature moves. But Styles needs to be careful. It took professional training for him to learn these moves. He learned how to avoid injuries. He's perfected the moves. He knows how to avoid seriously hurting himself and his opponents.

Styles uses many signature moves during the match. Halfway through, he tries the Calf Crusher. Styles pushes Ambrose to the mat. He sits on the floor by Ambrose's legs. He pulls Ambrose's calf up. Ambrose cries out and tries to get away. He manages to escape. But his knee is sore.

For his signature move, the Calf Crusher, Styles pulls on his opponent's leg.

Styles has many skills. He's worked hard to improve them. He is known for his airborne moves. One of these is the Phenomenal Forearm. He also does what he calls "crazy flips." People call him High-Flying AJ Styles.

Ambrose and Styles keep wrestling. They've fought for almost twenty-five minutes. Styles slams Ambrose onto the ground. He climbs to the top of the ropes. He jumps up high. He flips through the air. Then he lands hard on Ambrose. He almost pins him again.

Styles is sometimes called High-Flying AJ Styles because of the flips and jumps he uses in his wrestling matches.

THE PHENOMENAL
FOREARM

Right forearm set to strike opponent

Left arm extended

High leap into air off ropes

The match is coming to an end. Styles goes for another signature move. He pushes Ambrose's head down. He grabs Ambrose by the waist. Then he lifts him upside down. He's going to do a Styles Clash. Styles holds onto Ambrose's legs. He slams him to the ground. Ambrose is crushed against the mat. Styles pins him. The Styles Clash worked. He wins the match!

FUN FACT

AJ Styles was featured on the cover of the video game *WWE 2K19*.

For the Styles Clash, Styles lifts his opponent upside down and jumps down to the ground.

CHAPTER 4

In addition to wrestling for TNA and WWE, Styles wrestled for New Japan Pro-Wrestling.

A Phenomenal Career

Styles has had a long career. He has won many championships. He won eleven titles with TNA. He is considered one of the best TNA wrestlers. But he also holds titles from other wrestling companies. Styles competed for two years in Japan. He won two **international** titles. He joined WWE in 2016.

CAREER HIGHLIGHTS

1998

1998
AJ Styles debuts in NCW as Mr. Olympia.

1999

1999–2002
Styles wrestles with NWA Wildside and earns three world heavyweight championships and four tag team championships.

June 19, 2002
Styles debuts with TNA.

2002

2002–2013
Styles wins eleven titles with TNA, including Grand Slam, heavyweight, tag team, and X-Division championships.

2002–2006
While still wrestling for TNA, Styles also wins two titles with Ring of Honor.

2010

2010
Pro Wrestling Illustrated names AJ Styles the number-one wrestler in the world.

2014–2015
Styles wins two International Wrestling Grand Prix world heavyweight championships with New Japan Pro-Wrestling.

2014

2016

January 24, 2016
Styles debuts with WWE at Royal Rumble.

September 11, 2016
Styles defeats Dean Ambrose for his first WWE Championship.

2017

November 7, 2017
Styles defeats Jinder Mahal for his second WWE Championship. He holds the title for 371 days.

2017
Styles wins two WWE United States Championships.

Styles was excited to begin wrestling with WWE.
"I took the long route to get here," he said. He had years of
practice. He was ready for the new adventure. He wanted
to bring something special to WWE. But he was afraid the
fans wouldn't like him. He didn't need to worry, though. He
walked out for the first time at Royal Rumble. The WWE
fans cheered for him. "I could have melted. That's how
great it was," Styles said.

Styles loves wrestling for WWE, and he has many fans.

Styles has won four WWE titles. Two of them are WWE Championships. Once, he held that title for 371 days. Daniel Bryan beat Styles in November 2018.

FUN FACT

AJ Styles has won seven tag team titles.

He won the title from Styles. But Styles keeps wrestling. He can't wait for his next chance to be the champion.

AJ Styles joined forces with Shinsuke Nakamura for a tag team match in January 2018.

THE BOOK

After reading the book, it's time to think about what you learned. Try the following exercises to jumpstart your ideas.

THINK

THAT'S NEWS TO ME. How might news sources provide more information about AJ Styles's SummerSlam match with John Cena? What new information could you find in these articles? Where would you go to find these news sources?

CREATE

SHARPEN YOUR RESEARCH SKILLS. AJ Styles wrestled in school. Where could you go to learn more about high school and college wrestling? Create a research plan by writing a paragraph with your next steps for research.

SHARE

WHAT'S YOUR OPINION? AJ Styles is considered one of the greatest wrestlers from TNA. Do you agree with this? What evidence from the book supports your opinion? Share your opinion and evidence with a friend. Does your friend find your argument convincing?

GROW

DRAWING CONNECTIONS. Think about the human body and how its parts work. How do you think this concept connects with professional wrestling? Draw a diagram that shows how professional wrestling relates to the human body. How does learning about the human body help you to better understand professional wrestling?

RESEARCH NINJA

Visit *www.ninjaresearcher.com/0851* to learn how to take your research skills and book report writing to the next level!

RESEARCH

DIGITAL LITERACY TOOLS

SEARCH LIKE A PRO
Learn about how to use search engines to find useful websites.

FACT OR FAKE?
Discover how you can tell a trusted website from an untrustworthy resource.

TEXT DETECTIVE
Explore how to zero in on the information you need most.

SHOW YOUR WORK
Research responsibly— learn how to cite sources.

WRITE

GET TO THE POINT
Learn how to express your main ideas.

PLAN OF ATTACK
Learn prewriting exercises and create an outline.

DOWNLOADABLE REPORT FORMS

Further Resources

BOOKS

Black, Jake. *WWE Ultimate Superstar Guide*. WWE / DK
Publishing / Penguin Random House, 2018.

Borth, Teddy. *A.J. Styles: The Phenomenal One*. Abdo
Zoom, 2018.

Pantaleo, Steve, and Dean Miller. *WWE: Absolutely Everything
You Need to Know*. DK, 2017.

WEBSITES

FACTSURFER

Factsurfer.com gives you a safe,
fun way to find more information.

1. Go to www.factsurfer.com.

2. Enter "AJ Styles" into the search box and click 🔍.

3. Select your book cover to see a list of related websites.

Glossary

apron: The apron is the part of the mat that extends outside the ropes. AJ Styles slammed his opponent onto the apron.

bump: A bump is a hit or fall that knocks the opponent to the canvas. After his first bump, AJ Styles knew he could be a pro wrestler.

canvas: The canvas is the mat in a wrestling ring. The wrestler fell to the canvas.

international: Something is international if it takes place in or between more than one country. AJ Styles won an international title in Japan.

pinfall: A pinfall is when a wrestler holds an opponent's shoulders to the mat for an official count to three, resulting in a decision. AJ Styles won the match by pinfall.

promoter: A promoter is someone who helps organize a sporting event. A promoter gave AJ Styles his ring name.

sensational: Something is sensational when it causes a strong reaction from an audience or from the public. Pro wrestlers perform sensational moves to get the crowd cheering for them.

signature: Something is signature if it is unique to someone and people associate it with that person. Styles is known for signature moves that only he performs, like the Calf Crusher.

suplex: For a suplex, a wrestler locks his or her arms around an opponent's waist, then throws the opponent backward to the canvas. Styles leaned back to perform a suplex on Cena.

Index

PHOTO CREDITS

The images in this book are reproduced through the courtesy of: Christian Bertrand/Shutterstock Images, front cover; Yukio Hiraku/AFLO/Newscom, pp. 3, 22–23; Gwendoline Le Goff/Panoramic/Icon Sportswire, pp. 4, 4–5, 23; John Palmer/MediaPunch/IPX/AP Images, p. 6; Christian Bertrand/Shutterstock Images, pp. 8, 9, 19, 25, 30; JoeSAPhotos/Shutterstock Images, pp. 10–11; Olivier Andrivon/Icon Sport/Getty Images, pp. 12–13; Jerome Domine/Sipa USA/AP Images, pp. 14, 17, 20–21; Rob Tringali/Sports Illustrated/Set Number: X162079 TK1/Getty Images, pp. 16–17; JXSA/ZJAH/WENN.com/Jordan X/Alison Bailey/Newscom, p. 18; charnsitr/Shutterstock Images, p. 20; Red Line Editorial, p. 24 (timeline); Star Shooter/MediaPunch/IPX/AP Images, pp. 24 (belt), 26–27.

ABOUT THE AUTHOR

J. R. Kinley is a writer and artist. She is part of a wrestling family from Ohio in one of the top wrestling regions in the nation. Her husband, Shaun Kinley, former NCAA wrestler at The Ohio State University, coaches at the nationally ranked St. Edward High School. Together, they operate Kinley Studio.